## by Mark Stewart

ACKNOWLEDGMENTS

The editors wish to thank Gwen Torrence for her cooperation in preparing this book.
Thanks also to Integrated Sports International for their assistance.


PHOTO CREDITS

All photos courtesy AP/Wide World Photos, Inc. except the following:

Rob Tringali, Jr./Sports Chrome – 5 top, 27, 34, 42, 45
Sports Chrome – Cover, 30, 38
Tim O'Lett/Sports Chrome – 31, 35
Focus On Sports – 39
Dave Black/Fotosport – 5 center right, 6, 12, 46
University of Georgia – 19
Patrick Dennis/University of Georgia – 13, 16, 24 bottom left, 24 top center
Mark Stewart – 48


STAFF

*Project Coordinator:* John Sammis, Cronopio Publishing
*Series Design:* The Sloan Group
*Design and Electronic Page Makeup:* Jaffe Enterprises, Laura Marsala, Suzanne Murray,
    and Catherine Guarnieri


LIBRARY OF CONGRESS CATALOGING-IN-PUBLICATION DATA
Stewart, Mark
    Gwen Torrence / by Mark Stewart.
        p.  cm.  -- (Grolier all-pro biographies)
    Includes index.
    ISBN 0-516-20226-X (lib bdg.) -- ISBN 0-516-26046-4 (pbk.)
    1. Torrence, Gwen, 1965-  --Juvenile literature. 2. Women track and
field athletes--United States--Biography--Juvenile literature. I. Series
 GV697.T67S84  1996
 796.42'092--dc20
    [B]                                                          96-28951
                                                                    CIP
                                                                    AC

# Grolier ALL-PRO Biographies™

# Gwen Torrence

by
## Mark Stewart

## CHILDREN'S PRESS®
A Division of Grolier Publishing
New York • London • Hong Kong • Sydney
Danbury, Connecticut

# Contents

# Who Am I?

There is nothing complicated about being a winner. You have to work hard, believe in yourself, and look up to the right people. Luckily I discovered this in time to make the most out of the opportunities that came my way. I also know that it's never too late—or too early—to set goals and go after them. My name is Gwen Torrence, and this is my story . . . "

"It's never too late — or too early — to set goals."

# Growing Up

**D**orothy Torrence knew there was something special about her baby when little Gwen began walking at the young age of seven months. When she was just a year old, she was talking! Gwen always seemed to have somewhere to go and something to say. She was the youngest of the Torrence children—seven years younger than her nearest sibling, and seventeen years younger than her oldest. This meant there was always someone to play with Gwen and make sure that she was safe.

That was important, because her mother and father worked long hours. They wanted to save enough money to move from their cramped, two-bedroom apartment in Atlanta, Georgia, and buy a home with a backyard where their five children could play. Eventually, they were able to purchase a house in the suburb of Decatur, but not before her brother, Charles, was paralyzed during a game of football. If he had been playing on a regular field, the injury might not have occurred. But there was no such facility in the Atlanta projects, and kids often had to play on a dirt-rock field. A year later, tragedy struck the Torrence family again. Gwen's father suffered a stroke and died. Gwen was only nine years old, but she had already learned some hard lessons about life. "I began to see that things would not always go my way," she says.

Luckily, Gwen's friends and family were there to support her. Her best friend was a girl named Jackie. "We stayed close no matter what we went through," Gwen recalls. "And even if we got angry and said horrible things to each other, we never held grudges." Gwen's brother, Willie, also looked out for her. He would come to the rescue when she got into trouble and bought her little gifts when she was feeling sad.

School kept Gwen very busy during these troubling times. She liked math a lot, and she was not afraid to speak up in class. When she did not understand something, she asked her teachers for help. And when she was having a difficult time with a problem or project, she simply worked twice as hard until it was done. When it came to reading, she struggled at times but tried her best to keep up with the class. She knew how important it was to develop her reading skills. "A person cannot advance in life without knowledge," says Gwen. "You have to learn to read so you can learn as much as you can."

When Gwen enrolled at Columbia High School, she was like most other kids her age. She enjoyed hanging out with her friends and listening to music, and she loved to dance. Some of the students at her school were beginning to experiment with drugs and alcohol, but Gwen chose not to. "I was able to keep away from bad influences by looking deep within myself and asking myself if it was good for me," she says. "That's what you have to do whenever you are trying to decide if something's right or wrong. Ask yourself, 'Will this make me a better person? Will this hurt someone? How will I feel about this later on?' Answer these questions before you act."

Gwen was different from her friends in one important respect: she could run like the wind. Yet she had little interest in sports and did not even go out for the school's track team in her freshman year. That did not sit well with her physical education teacher, Coach Ray Bonner. He once saw Gwen outrun one of the fastest boys in the school, and he was convinced she could be a champion. One day, he asked her to run the 220-yard dash. Wearing street clothes and low-heeled shoes, Gwen flew down the track. When Coach Bonner looked at his stopwatch he could hardly believe his eyes. Gwen had just shattered the state record!

Coach Bonner soon became an important figure in Gwen's life. He convinced her to join the team, saying it would be a tragedy to let her natural ability go to waste. "Ray Bonner was my favorite teacher," says Gwen. "He not only introduced me to the sport, he stressed the importance of education and made sure

I kept up with my studies. I knew I could not do one without doing the other."

At first, Gwen was too shy to train with the other girls, so she would practice on her own after they had gone home. Soon, she was winning everything in sight. In tenth grade, Gwen was the state champion in the 100-yard dash and the 200-yard dash. In 11th grade, she won these events again. And in her senior year she was state champ in the 100 and 200 a third consecutive time, earning All-America honors

Gwen was a state champion in many high-school track competitions.

in the process. Gwen's best time in the 100 was 11.9 seconds. After graduation, Gwen competed in the Junior Olympics and won two gold medals.

Gwen received a scholarship offer from the University of Georgia. Initially, she declined. Her grades were not very good, and she did not feel ready for college. Besides, Gwen wanted to be a hair stylist and did not see what being a college sprinter had to do with that. But Coach Bonner reminded her about the importance of education. If she planned to make something of herself in life, he maintained, a college diploma would be the key. Eventually, Gwen agreed, and she accepted the scholarship from the University of Georgia in nearby Athens.

Gwen decided to attend the University of Georgia.

# College

wen Torrence had been a star on the athletic field in high school, but her performance in the classroom was well below average. No one questioned whether she was bright enough to succeed in college, but her test scores were so low that she could only gain acceptance at Georgia under the Developmental Studies program. Gwen would be allowed to take courses and run track at the university for one year. If she failed at either, she would be sent back home to Decatur.

Gwen passed all of her courses and proved to be an excellent student. For the first time in her life, she was reading books and writing papers . . . and loving every minute of it. Gwen did well in her freshman track season, too. She qualified for the finals in the 100 and 200 at the 1984 NCAA Indoor Championships. She did so well that she was invited to the U.S. Olympic Trials.

In 1985, Gwen anchored the U. S. team in the 400-meter relay at the World University Games.

# Years

**I**ncredibly, Gwen did not go. She told Georgia track coach Lewis Gainey that she did not feel good enough to be in the Olympics. "I thought I was too young," she says. "Also, at that point in my life, track was a way to get an education. I certainly did not think it would be my career."

Gwen's times improved dramatically over the next two years. At the 1986 Millrose Games, she beat Olympic gold medalist Evelyn Ashford in the

**Gwen beats Evelyn Ashford to set a record at the 1986 Millrose Games.**

55 meters with a time of 6.57 seconds—the fastest ever recorded in the history of the competition. Later that year, she won the NCAA title in the 55 meters. Track people were beginning to notice Gwen, and she was starting to gain the confidence she would need to make track her career. "I had begun to realize that track-and-field was opening a lot of doors for me," Gwen recalls.

A lot of doors were opening for Gwen. Unlike many college athletes, she took her education very seriously. Gwen studied early childhood education, and she planned to work with children with disabilities when she graduated. When she was not going to class or traveling to track meets, she could often be found spending time with children who had various physical or mental disabilities. By her senior year, Gwen had become one of the most capable students on campus, and she easily made the dean's list. Meanwhile, her track career was really taking off. At the 1987 NCAA Championships, Gwen

At Georgia, Gwen was a four-time NCAA champion and a 12-time All-American.

A four-time All-American in the 55 and 100 meters, Gwen Torrence turned in some great performances during the NCAA Championships:

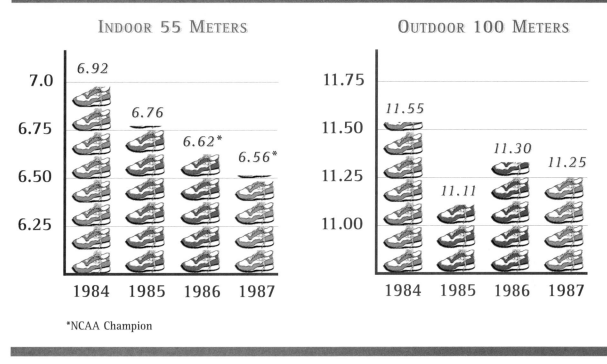

INDOOR 55 METERS

OUTDOOR 100 METERS

*NCAA Champion

ran wild. She won all three sprint events—the 55, the 100, and the 200—then won three gold medals at the World University Games in Zagreb, Yugoslavia. With the 1988 Olympics just around the corner, Gwen was ready to move to the top of her sport.

**Gwen celebrates her win in the 100 meters at the 1987 World University Games.**

# The Story

**G**wen Torrence was practically unbeatable heading into 1988. In the Millrose Games that year, she won her 33rd race in a row, defeating Evelyn Ashford. That victory put Gwen in the spotlight during the Olympics in Seoul, South Korea. The sprints were expected to be a showdown between her and Ashford, but Florence Griffith-Joyner stunned the world by winning both the 100 and 200, setting new Olympic records in each. Gwen finished fifth in the 100 and sixth in the 200. The following year, she had a son with Manley Waller, her husband and coach. Manley Jr. took up most of Gwen's time in 1990, but she was determined to make it back to the 1992 Olympics and "go for the gold."

# Continues

Gwen beats Evelyn Ashford to the tape.

Although Gwen did not medal in the 1988 Olympics, she was proud just to be in the finals. "I knew in times to come if I kept working hard I had the ability to strike gold in the 1992 Olympics."

In 1991, Gwen returned to the track. She entered the World Championships and finished second to Germany's Katrin Krabbe, who was later banned from the sport for using performance-enhancing drugs. In 1992, Gwen won the 100 and 200 in the Olympic Trials, and again was one of the favorites when the U.S. track team arrived in Barcelona, Spain, for the Summer Olympics. But there misfortune struck again. Despite turning in her best time ever in the 100, Gwen finished fourth. After the race, she was angry and disappointed. Gail Devers had won the gold medal fair and square, maintained Gwen, but she suspected that some other runners had improved their performances by using drugs. It did not seem fair to her that she played by the rules while others did not. Although her charges were dismissed by track-and-field officials, Gwen stood by her claims.

Gwen found herself in the center of a growing controversy. She was hounded by reporters, who tried to get her to "name names." They wanted her to reveal the names of the athletes she suspected of using drugs. This made it very hard to prepare for the 200 meters, but Gwen just increased her focus and concentration. When the gun sounded in the final heat, she burst out of the blocks and stormed to victory. Winning the gold medal was the proudest moment in her career.

**T**wo days later, Gwen was in the spotlight again as a member of the U.S. relay team. She had been chosen to run the anchor leg, which meant that she would sprint the final 100 meters. Gwen took the baton about six feet behind Russia's Irina Privalova. Gwen squeezed every ounce of speed out of her body to make up the difference, then found just a little more to edge her by 1/20th of a second for her second gold medal. Before she left Barcelona, Gwen won a third medal—this one a silver—as a member of the 4x400 relay team.

The 1992 Olympic 4x100 relay gold medalists were (left to right) Gwen Torrence, Carlette Guidry, Esther Jones, and Evelyn Ashford.

fter such an incredible performance, some people expected Gwen to retire. But she already had her eye on the 1996 Olympics, which would be held in her hometown of Atlanta. Between 1992 and 1996, she continued to dominate at every distance. Her goal? To win the gold in the 100 meters—the one Olympic medal that had eluded her. "There is something special about the 100 meters," she smiles. "Everyone wants to be the world's fastest woman."

Gwen sprints to victory at the 1996 Mobil Championships in Atlanta.

Gwen (#66) anchors the U.S. relay team at the 1994 Goodwill Games in Russia.

# Timeline

**1987: Becomes NCAA 100-meter champion**

**1988: Wins 34th consecutive race at Millrose Games**

**1986: Captures her first NCAA spring championship with win in 55 meters**

1992: Wins one silver and two gold medals at Barcelona Olympics

1996: Captures 100-meter championship in Atlanta

1994: Wins 4x100-meter relay gold medal at Goodwill Games

# Track

In 1996, Gwen won the first 100-meter competition ever held in Atlanta's Olympic Stadium, when she broke the tape with a spectacular time of 10.85 seconds.

Gwen is usually the skinniest runner in any of her competitions.

# Action!

Gwen was surprised when she won the 100-meter race at the 1992 Olympic Trials.

**G**wen surprised even herself by winning the 100 meters at the 1992 Olympic Trials despite a painful knee injury. "I lost all form and just ran desperately for the line," she remembers. "Third place would have done me just fine!"

**I**f runners were judged on size alone, Gwen would not stand a chance. "I'm always the skinniest sprinter in the field," she says.

**G**wen ran the second leg of the 4 x 400-meter relay in an amazing 49.8 seconds at the 1992 Olympics. Many felt she should have anchored the team, but Gwen was just happy to have the chance to compete. "It would have been nice to anchor," she says. "But I never asked. Hey, I was honored just to be running four events."

**I**n 1992, Gwen achieved her dream by winning gold medals as an individual performer and as a member of the U.S. team. "Winning those medals at the 1992 Olympics was the proudest moment of my career."

Evelyn Ashford, Esther Jones, Gwen, and Carlette Guidry celebrate their 1992 victory in the Olympic 4x100-meter relay.

Gwen reacts to the news that she was disqualified after winning the 200 meters at the 1995 World Championships.

At the 1995 World Championships, Gwen was denied a victory over archrival Merlene Ottey in the 200 meters when she mistakenly stepped on the line of her lane. She gained a measure of revenge by edging Ottey for the gold medal in the final leg of the 4x100-meter relay.

Gwen enjoyed competing in Atlanta. "It's nice my mother gets to see what I do when I 'go to the office,'" she jokes.

The sprinter Gwen most admired during her early years was Evelyn Ashford. "I respected Evelyn more than I could ever tell her, because we were competitors."

**G**wen's breakthrough year was 1987, when she won NCAA titles in the 55, 100, and 200, then captured gold medals at the World University Games in 100 and 200.

**G**wen made the U.S. Olympic team for the first time in 1988, finishing fifth in the 100 meters and sixth in the 200 meters.

Gwen streaks to a 1992 Olympic gold medal in the 200 meters, the "proudest moment" of her life.

# Reaching

**G**wen Torrence draws strength from her fans. With their love, support, and courage, she is able to do what it takes to push herself to be the best.

"This young man named Joey used to write me all the time and I wrote him, too. He had cancer, and I think it was hereditary, because his mother died of cancer. In his letters he would write, 'I am surprised I woke up this morning.' I felt like—as sick as he was—he always found the strength to write me, and write me of his support for me. From that moment on I realized that, although track has been good to me, it is not everything in life. I should be more thankful for waking up each morning with the strength to work out."

Gwen Torrence knows that young athletes look to her for inspiration, and she is happy to share her training tips and experiences with them. Gwen believes that the more people

# Out

International crowds, like the one here in Brussels, appreciate Gwen's victories.

understand her, the more they will learn about what it takes to be a champion both on and off the track.

"Passing along my knowledge and advice is important because it allows young athletes to hear that I have traveled the same road as them. I have faced the same pressures and temptations, and survived. I also think it lets them see that I am human—not a perfect person, but a good person."

# HOW DOES

# She Do It?

**B**eing a world-class sprinter takes speed, strength, and timing. Being an Olympic champion takes something more. According to Gwen Torrence, the difference between winning the gold and coming up empty is all in your head.

"I take enormous pride in my ability to concentrate. From the moment I settle into the starting blocks until I break the tape, I am totally focused on one thing: running an absolutely perfect race."

At the starting blocks or in the middle of a race, Gwen is all concentration.

# The Grind

Gwen Torrence has been called outspoken, stubborn, and controversial. Indeed, she admits that she could probably improve her relationship with the press, the public, and her fellow runners. She also knows that her reputation may have cost her a commercial endorsement or two. Gwen knows how important it is for an athlete to present a good public image, but she also knows that she would rather quit running than try to be something that she is not.

"The toughest thing about being a well-known athlete is remembering to be myself instead of pretending to be something others want me to be."

# Career

Gwen Torrence has established herself as one of the finest sprinters in history. She has worked long and hard to perfect her technique and develop her powers of concentration. This gives her an edge over other runners, who must rely on raw speed to win races. When Gwen runs a race, she uses her whole body from head to toe. Over the years, she has proved to be as versatile as she is exciting. Gwen excels whether she is running indoors or outdoors, and is as tough to beat at 200 meters as she is at 50 meters. Her fabulous "homecoming" at the 1996 Summer Olympics in Atlanta was one of the biggest sports stories of the year.

Gwen was nicknamed "The Pink Panther" for her trademark running suits.

# Highlights

**G**wen was an All-American and three-time Georgia state champion sprinter while in high school.

**G**wen's first victory against top international competition came in the 200 meters at the 1987 Pan Am Games.

Gwen streaks to victory in the 100-meter 1992 Olympic Trials.

In 1987, Gwen recorded a time of 6.56 seconds in the 55 meters. No one has ever topped that mark.

One of Gwen's biggest victories came in the 200 meters at the 1991 U.S. Nationals. She won this event again in 1992, 1993, and 1995.

Gwen edges out
Russia's best sprinter,
Irina Privalova,
at the 1994
Goodwill games.

**G**wen was the 1994 U.S. Indoor
champion in the 60 meters.

**I**n 1992, Gwen captured gold medals in the 200 meters
and the 4x100-meter relay during the Summer
Olympics in Barcelona.

Gwen, Evelyn Ashford, and Carlette Guidry
(left to right) celebrate their relay victory
at the 1992 Olympics in Barcelona.

Gwen sets an American
indoor record for the
200 meters with a time
of 22.74 seconds.

Gwen wins gold at
the 1995 World
Championships.

Gwen also won a gold in the 4x100-relay at the World Championships. Here she celebrates with Carlette Guidry, Celena Monde-Milner, and Chryste Gaines.

n 1995, Gwen won the 100-meter championships at both the U.S. Nationals and the World Championships.

# Numbers

Name: Gwendolyn Torrence

Weight: 127 lbs.

Born: June 12, 1965

College: University of Georgia

Height: 5' 8"

Here are Gwen's best times heading into the 1996 season:

| Event | Time | Year |
|---|---|---|
| 50 Meters | 6.05 | 1991 |
| 55 Meters | 6.56* | 1987 |
| 60 Meters | 7.02 | 1995 |
| 100 Meters | 10.82 | 1994 |
| 200 Meters | 21.72 | 1992 |
| 400 Meters | 49.64 | 1992 |

\* World Record

# Glossary

**COMMERCIAL ENDORSEMENT** representing a company's product through the media

**CONSECUTIVE** several events that follow one after another

**CONTROVERSY** a disagreement; an argument

**CRUCIAL** very important; significant

**DEAN'S LIST** college level honor roll for excellence in education

**ELUDED** escaped; missed; foiled

**FACILITY** something that is built, installed, or established to serve a particular purpose

**NCAA** National Collegiate Athletic Association

PERFORMANCE-ENHANCING
  DRUGS drugs such as
  steroids that temporarily
  improve the user's
  performance but are illegal
  because the side effects
  are often deadly

PROJECTS a public
  housing development
  often consisting of
  several look-alike houses
  or apartments

REBOUNDED bounced back;
  recovered

SCHOLARSHIP money given
  to a student to help pay for
  schooling

STAMINA strength;
  endurance; staying power

VERSATILE having the ability
  to excel in many different
  areas; multi-talented

# Index

## About The Author

Mark Stewart grew up in New York City in the 1960s and 1970s—when the Mets, Jets, and Knicks all had championship teams. As a child, Mark read everything about sports he could lay his hands on. Today, he is one of the busiest sportswriters around. Since 1990, he has written close to 500 sports stories for kids, including profiles on more than 200 athletes, past and present. A graduate of Duke University, Mark served as senior editor of *Racquet*, a national tennis magazine, and was managing editor of *Super News*, a sporting goods industry newspaper. He is the author of every Grolier All-Pro Biography.